How to Heal

From a

Narcissistic

Relationship

How to Heal From a Narcissistic Relationship

By

Nancy Sungyun

How to Heal From a Narcissistic relationship

By Nancy Sungyun

Copyright © 2020 by Nancy Sungyun

Published and distributed in the United States.

Printed in the United States of America

Copyright page

Dedication

This book is dedicated to all who have suffered narcissistic abuse.

Table of content

How to Heal From a Narcissistic Relationship

"The emotion that can break your heart is sometimes the very one that heals it..."

— Nicholas Sparks

Introduction

How I learned to put up with abusive relationships

My childhood was a perfect petri dish for growing up to be a co-dependent adult who would someday be perfect for an abusive narcissist to pluck and use for their needs and wants.

There was constant and passionate disdain for who I was while people demanded I do anything and everything with whatever resources and power I had. I had to do all that I could, and I did. I did it to get the little semblance of affection that I possibly could as a little girl. I did all the housework, cooking, cleaning, laundering, anything that I could do. Working for the barest amount of affection like I did, of course, helped me to be the perfect co-dependent partner for my future relationships.

*

On my first day of middle school, I put on my brand new uniform, big enough to grow into for the next four years. I was excited. I looked down at the shoes that I had worn — I cannot remember now exactly how long — for long enough for them to have holes at the edges revealing my white socks. I instantly felt shame, fearing my new friends in school would think badly of me. But, I still had some hope and was excited about wearing the brand new uniform that I had been looking forward to most of my elementary years. We all did. The girls with those middle school uniforms were older. There was a kind of status you gained by wearing those dark blue uniforms with large white triangular collars. I longed for them. We all wanted them.

For me personally, it also had another benefit. I would not have to dress any worse than any other girls in a uniform. I would look equal to other girls who were wearing expensive, cute clothes and shoes. I had looked forward to that as well.

I looked up from my uniform and saw the disgust on my adoptive father's face as he said the following words that I have never forgotten. He said, "No matter how good and beautiful clothing is, when you put it on an ugly hanger, the clothing becomes ugly."

In my mind, I thought, "Maybe it's because of the torn shoes that I look ugly. Maybe it's because the uniform was three years' too big for me." But I could not say such things to him or ever disagree with anything that he said for fear of the painful and scary consequences that would have followed. I just felt incredibly ugly, worthless and very, very small.

I did not sense a tinge of anger in his voice when he said it. It was in one of his very gentle-sounding voices, with a little, casual smile and even bit of pity. That was one of the mildest of his many cruel acts toward me.

I think back and think, "Gosh, I was just a small child. I remember how scared I was always living with them. I remember how frightened I was when he said that to me, fearing that he would beat me for being so ugly, wishing I could be pretty so that I could escape the scary thing that I feared may come at me. I used to wish that I could just wish away what I looked like, what I sounded like, what I was like so that they would spare me the punishments that such a creature like me deserved."

*

And, all the while, I saw my adoptive mother being controlled and willingly docile. In my future narcissistic relationship, I would play that role out as well.

*

From my abusive narcissist parents, I learned that I was not lovable, and so I deserved pretty much nothing good instead I should be resigned to receive the bad. So I walked through life living up to that standard that I learned so well. No matter what I was learning intellectually about healthy relationships and aiming to only find people who treat me well, without fail I defaulted to abusive relationships characterised by poor treatment and emotional abandonment. It looked as if I would be stuck with this condition no matter how hard I tried to escape it.

*

The universe seemed to have had a different plan for me, however. If I was willing, that is. I needed to find the way and it was going to be an interesting, startling, confusing, and painful journey ending with the greatest gift.

I would fall madly in love with, experience utter confusion, and be baffled daily by a man who displayed all the typical symptoms of narcissism. He was the perfect storm of emotional abusiveness, emotional abandonment, gaslighting, emotional disregard, the constant need to be right , devoid of empathy, and a need for complete control.

What I went through with his narcissism was the very thing that I had to have in my life to show me what I had to learn. I had to shed all the stuff that I learned from my narcissistic adoptive mom and dad and was hiding from: the dysfunctional beliefs, the self-assessment, and the lack of self-worth.

*

Another way of looking at it would be that I learned while working to heal correctly from the narcissistic relationship that I had, how to heal the injuries that I gained from my narcissistic adoptive parents. And, by doing that, I would conquer my world.

I learned that I had such low self-esteem and a lack of self-value because of my childhood. What I learned from my childhood made me not trust my own perspective on the hurtful and confusing things that happened in that relationship with a narcissistic man, who strangely used to remind me of both my adoptive mother and father.

The journey I had to take on this healing process showed me how to shake off the stubborn set of beliefs that I needed to work through and exorcise. But, when I met him, fell in love with his love bombing, and when I endured the devaluation and discarding, I had no idea that going through all of it would be the catalyst to my healing and awakening. Healing from the painful heartbreak in the right way would result in addressing my long-time life companions: insecurities, fears, low self-esteem, low self-trust, and low self-value.

Healing myself from that relationship properly meant I had to overcome the pain that I had endured in my childhood. So, that's what I did.

*

It took me a long time to finally become the person that I wanted to be, but I finally am the person that I have always wanted to be. It is a wonder, this life, the possibility to heal is endless, and the joy you gain from the healing is limitless.

Now that I have gained so many necessary tools that have helped me on my path to emotional mastery, I spontaneously gain more tools. The fear of 'what ifs' and 'what if not's' no longer dominates my mind. I now know that the waves of life come in and go out, but the calm in between, the beauty that I get to create, the messages that I gain and teach, and all the emotions involved in this thing called life are all just as they should be.

Getting to this place where life is so different and but also so similar but I have changed so much from how I was then, the person who was abused, is beyond my wildest dreams.

*

In this book, I am going to share with you the powerful keys that I gained: the tools, the gems, the boons that I found on my journey. They can now become yours and you too can become a person who no longer puts up with abuse from a narcissist or anyone else.

"So it's true, when all is said and done, grief is the price we pay for love."
— E.A. Bucchianeri

Chapter 1 - What you must do first

Suppose you have just experienced heartbreak, no matter whether it was a good relationship or a bad relationship. In that case, you must fully allow yourself room to grieve being compassionate and empathetic with yourself.

There is indeed a benefit to being around unconditionally loving, empathetic, and compassionate people, but there is no substitute for that love, empathy, and compassion dwelling inside yourself. After all, it is your inner world that you take with you everywhere you go. And no matter how loving, empathetic, and compassionate others might be to you, you will still be influenced most powerfully by yourself.

Many studies have followed women and men who deal with heartbreak. These studies have shown that most women tend to experience more pain than men after a heartbreak. They have found that women tend to allow themselves to feel and move through the experience. At the same time, many men often skip right to a new relationship, and, therefore, women are more likely to fully heal and move on as healthier people. The men, however, often do not fully get over the loss of the relationship. This outcome strongly indicates the importance of fully grieving the loss so that you can deeply heal, and move forward in your life.

In my break-up with my narcissist, I had the most fantastic growing and healing experience. But, what I did not do in the early part of my break-up was fully grieve the loss of my relationship. I was so busy learning, studying, researching, and building healing, positive habits into my life that I skipped over some parts of grieving, having jumped too quickly into self-growth work as well as my writing.

The result was that after quite a bit of time had passed, I found myself still having emotional reactions when he would contact me in one form or another. I had built a habit of practicing healthy boundaries, which helped a lot, but I still felt sadness or a disturbance in my emotional balance. I wondered why it was that even though I was clear about not wanting any connection with him, I still felt such a profound sense of loss. I realized that I had not fully grieved because I had been so excited about working on myself, building myself, and gaining more knowledge and skills.

What I had to do was pull myself back to the moments of the heartbreak, guide myself through the steps of compassionately acknowledging my loss, and give myself empathy for the pain of that loss. I finally cried, which I remember thinking I wasn't doing enough during the early phase. So, I finally cried and I finally gave myself some well-deserved empathy. I felt the feelings of loss without judgment of any kind. It took that ritual of honoring my pain, accepting that there was a loss, and giving myself compassion, for me to finally fully let go.

As you go through grieving, healing, learning, and growing to reach for your higher self, you must consistently provide yourself with empathy-filled compassion. I will be going over in this book the steps you need to properly heal so that you can come out of it on the other side not just healed, but a healthier and more capable person in all areas of your life.

As you begin to study the healing and emotional skills that you need, you must grieve — grieve now and grieve fully — so that you can let go of that relationship and move on to your whole life.

So, with your loving inner environment as a consistent background, follow the next steps mindfully and with love:

- You fully acknowledge the loss for yourself. You do this with empathy and compassion.

- Don't fear the pain. Doing that only makes your experience worse. When you just move through the pain, you get to see it for what it is, just sensations.

- Honor your memories and experiences. Do not engage in negative self-talk about what you experienced in the relationship.

- Do your best to take loving care of yourself (visit the self-care chapters of this book if you'd like.)

- Spend some time in a quiet and relaxing space to affirm feelings and thoughts that come up for you.

- When you have painful feelings that come up relating to the heartbreak, stop if you are able, sit down or lie down, and clear your headspace to feel. Then give yourself empathy and compassion for your pain.

- Know that you are going to be ok. I promise you will be ok. And, just so you know, you are ok right now. Your feelings do not define your life. The fact that you are on a healing path means you are on a beautiful life journey. Just as I have discovered this powerfully myself, you will do the same, and that is worth everything.

When you go through these steps, making sure to honor the process, you can then fully move on and move toward the life you deserve.

"What happens when people open their hearts?"

"They get better."

— Haruki Murakami

Chapter 2 - What your heartbreak means

Heartbreak is powerful. Our self-esteem plummets. We even lose the ability to think clearly and logically. Our IQ lowers. We become less than capable thinkers, which causes our perceptions to be less than reliable. Our foundation shakes, and we get thrown off balance while we cannot think ourselves out of the painful situation.

When we break away from an abusive relationship, it is often worse.

On top of the usual heartbreak, the abused partner goes through the added pain of withdrawal from the trauma bonding.

In effect, there is a close connection between the very reason why we stayed in the inappropriate relationship that had made us so unhappy and the reason why we are hurting more intensely than if we were feeling the loss of a connection that did not have a trauma bonding component to it.

If you've had many bad relationships or only bad ones in your life, healing yourself properly from this heartbreak will set your life right in the ways that you have always needed to do to be authentically happy.

Doctors sometimes re-break your bones so that they heal right. This heartbreak of yours can be that re-break of your emotional self so that you can set your life right and move forward.

You will, after doing this self-work, know how to find relationships that are empowering and authentic. Most importantly you will heal your heart, find your best self, find your best life, find your genuine happiness, and even get on your life's true path.

By healing from this heartbreak the right way, you will gain the ability to fix your whole life in ways that you have not known how to do before. You will find happiness in ways that you have never known before. You will experience self-confidence and self-acceptance in ways that you have never really known before. You will feel more consistently comfortable in your own skin, liking and loving who you are in ways you have never done before. You will know how to be responsible for your own feelings and your own emotional well-being, learning to let go of things that don't serve you. You will know how to discern between emotional rights and emotional wrongs.

If you've been putting up with bad relationships, there is a reason why. You learned somewhere along the way during your childhood that you were unworthy of safety, real comfort, feeling enough, and, crucially, unworthy of love. During that process, you, as a child, learned that you deserve no respect, neglect, and harsh treatment or even abuse. You would have determined that you were not worthy of the love: you were not enough and you had to earn your keep.

When you felt a hunger for love and deep loneliness as a child, you would not have known that you deserved better. You would have come to believe that you must be bad. The abusive adults in your life would have shown you that regularly by both saying it to you directly and by ignoring your needs. You, as a little child, would have had no way of knowing that they were wrong.

Being mistreated would have become normal. You were being taught that you deserve no better.

You are heartbroken. You feel bad, but you wonder why you feel as badly as you do because your partner did not make you happy when you were with him or her. You were very unhappy while you were in the relationship. So, you ask yourself why it is that you feel so badly. Why do you have this phantom feeling of missing your ex-partner?

As I have said before, all of it is connected. All the seemingly illogical reasons why this is happening to you right now are connected.

When you process your heartbreak the right way, you will come to understand why. You will also come to resolve the very thing in your life that you have needed to address. You will become better, healthier, and happier. You will begin learning how to be the best version of you. How do I know this to be true? Let me tell you what happened to me.

I have been a student of self-healing since I was sixteen years old. I struggled and fought to learn every healing method that I could through traditional education, alternative life coaching, and countless books. All of my studies finally came to fruition when I went through a painful heartbreak about two years ago. The change and the calm in me about the ebb and flow of my life is lovely. My healing has forever altered me and I know that if I can do it, anyone can.

I have always believed and continue to believe that the first step toward making a positive difference in the world for anyone is in becoming a self-loving, wholehearted, and authentic human being. When I am in that state of being, I am kinder, loving, and genuinely giving. As that kind of person, I sit in the most potent place to do good for my world. If our society were full of happier self-loving, self-accepting people, we would have a much more joyful and loving world.

As a happier human being, you will be genuinely useful for all those who are in your life, all those who come in contact with you, and, in turn, your whole world. You will make a positive difference in the world without even trying. And the effortless positivity will spread across the globe.

I can imagine a world filled with people who are genuinely happy and at peace. I want to live in that world. How about you? Would you like to be healed from your heartbreak the right way and, by doing so, make a genuine positive difference in your life and the lives of those whom you touch? If you do, then come with me.

If you could pay with your time to learn how to set your life right, to heal from this heartbreak and other heartbreaks in your life, how many days would you invest in doing it? Would you be willing to spend the next eight weeks of your life building a habit to set yourself on the right path?

Eight weeks is long enough to practice and establish new and positive emotional habits. That's what happened to me. It not only helped put me on a healing path from my heartbreak but, more powerfully, it has transformed who I am and continues to do so in ways that I could never have imagined.

I have inner resources now that I never knew I could have. I know how to feel happy. I know how to process difficult emotions, which I had no clue how to resolve on my own before. I know how to rely on myself to solve difficult emotions in ways that I had never known about before. I know how to accept and love myself unconditionally. I know how to face things that I had never known how to face before. I finally know how to be comfortable in my own skin in ways that I had never known how to before. When I do have moments where I forget, I can realise it on my own once I recognize the emotional conflict. I know how to be emotionally self-reliant in ways that I had never known how to do before.

I will share with you what I did and why it works. I will also share with you things that I learned in the latter part of my bootcamp that you could use on the first day so that your bootcamp process is easier and even more fruitful for you than it was for me.

Doing the eight-week bootcamp will put you on the road of healing from your recent heartbreak. It will also start building in you a positive habit that will heal the rest of your life. You will be killing two very annoying birds with one powerful stone. Let's get started!

What you will need to do next:

Make a clear decision that you are going to heal from this in the right way. You are going to improve your whole life so you will no longer put up with what is not working. Be clear that you are going to become a person who lives to be their best, always. Be sure that you want to be the best version of you, discover your true potential, and live fully with a healed heart.

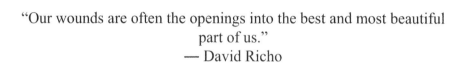

"Our wounds are often the openings into the best and most beautiful part of us."
— David Richo

Chapter 3 - What it means to truly heal

"Please tell me when this pain will stop. When will it stop? How long before I can stop feeling this pain? I just want my healing. I want this pain to stop." My client Patty continued to repeat those agonizing words during our first session. I could almost see the pain drops oozing from her every pore. She was suffering, and the pain was engulfing her.

She had just been discarded by a narcissist who had been emotionally abusive to her for several years. She had lost contact with just about everyone in her family and friends because of his intense dislike of them. Being a people pleaser, she eventually gave in to all of his demands. She had quit her job because he didn't like her commuting such a long distance from home. He said he was worried about her safety. She went to everything that his business demanded because she was needed. She was the only one that he trusted to set up his events the way he wanted.

She was happy to have him need her help a bit less in the last month of their relationship before he broke up with her. She could finally do some things for herself. When he broke the news that he was in love with someone else, her ex told her angrily that it was because Patty had gained 20 lbs and had become argumentative, proving that she was not loyal to him and he could no longer trust her. He followed it up with, "Thank God, I finally found the perfect woman for me now." He seemed utterly confused by her hurt and asked that she move out ASAP because her getting emotional about it was too much for him to handle. He said that he would have given her a month to move, but he could not put up with her being so emotional. Her ex also told her he was glad that he decided to dump her since he knew now just how selfish she was because of how she was reacting to him falling in love. If she loved him, she would have been happy for him, he argued.

When she came to work with me, she had been trying to get over him but was failing at it: scrolling through his social media and feeling even more horrible seeing his photos with his new girlfriend, looking so happy.

She was in desperate and great pain.

As Patty began her healing journey and started doing the exercises that I describe in Chapter 11, she could see that not all her deep pain was coming from the heartbreak.

Piggybacking on the rejection and heartbreak that she was suffering was the emotional experience that she experienced as a child. The rejection and heartbreak of her current situation echoes the rejection and heartbreak from her childhood.

What she needed to do to heal herself was to put her focus on freeing herself from the dysfunction that she had learned to become a part of: the very reason why she had been willing to be in a relationship that was making her so unhappy.

The complicated relationship that she had just come out of had elements for her she needed to explore so that she did not not enter another abusive relationship in the future. She needed to repair the very thing that allowed her to stay with a man who abused her. She would need to do some profound self-discovery to heal her old wounds.

One of the pains that she had to heal was her father coming and going from her and her mother's life, coming back home in between girlfriends and once even marrying someone else, then returning to her mother after his divorce. When he was around, he seemed to adore Patty, though not her mother, but once he was gone, Patty and her mother would both be ghosted by him again.

To heal herself, she had to give her child-self compassion and empathy. She acknowledged the pain of rejection that she suffered from her father when he would leave again. She forgave herself for the guilt that she felt when her father would shower her with love, affection, and gifts while being cold, cruel, and even physically abusive to her mother when he was drunk.

Over the years, she carried guilt for enjoying his attention while knowing that he was treating her mother differently. She felt guilt and shame for not having stood up for her mother.

While doing her healing work, she realized that she was only a child who needed and desperately wanted to be loved by her father. She was only a child and didn't have the power to — nor was she supposed to —rescue her mother. She realized that as a child her only job was to be loved and be protected, which her father and her mother failed to provide.

Two months into our work together, she texted me one morning to let me know that she applied for a job that she thought was far out of her reach. She said that she did it just because she was afraid of getting rejected. Fear of rejection had influenced too many decisions in her life, she said, and she was determined to change that. She knew she had a high chance of not getting hired for that job, but she didn't want to not do something out of fear of rejection anymore. She also began talking more candidly about her father with her mother.

After four months of our work together, she began volunteering at a women's shelter once a week. Patty wanted to help other women who were going through what she and her mother had gone through. She also had a feeling that she was going to heal and grow a lot by helping those women.

Here's the thing: when you see that this pain in your life is about more than you, you truly began your healing path, which means you solve two compelling problems simultaneously.

As you heal yourself, you are improving the world.

The pain you are experiencing can be the most powerful opportunity: a chance for you to see something in your life that you have always needed to see and heal to be able to significantly improve your progress. You will tackle something that has been a roadblock for you for far too long, and fuel yourself to reach the potential that you had never really even known you had.

In the end, your pain could be, and is very likely to be, something that you have much to learn from. Let it be your hero's journey.
According to Joseph Campbell, a "hero's journey" is a journey you take to resolve a problem in your life. When you fix your problem, you

gain a skill set that will help you solve your future problems. The ability that you learn is a boon. You are then supposed to use the boon to improve your world by sharing it.

Deepak Chopra echoes that sentiment, if in a bit of a different way, by teaching that Karma is not payment for your deeds, good or bad, but rather it is a challenge in your life that you are to tackle so that you can then use what you learn to teach the rest of the world.

I have personally found this to be the case. As I will explore throughout the book, the experiences that I have had personally confirm this to be the case.

There is no better way to heal from pain, challenges, or roadblocks than by doing it in a way that gives you gifts from the painful experience. It is much better than merely falling victim to the unpleasant incident, no matter the problematic episode.

My client Patty realized that she was repeating the event that happened to her mother and her when she was only a child in her adult life. Her healing finally began when she turned her focus on herself to look for healing and the gift. The experience with her narcissist was a gift that allowed her to heal her childhood trauma:, her father's rejection, her guilt toward her mother, and, finally, the rejection that she felt from her mother due to the constant emotional turmoil over her father.

By the end of our work, when Patty began to volunteer at the women's shelter to help other abused women on their own journeys healing from trauma, I knew she was well on her way. She not only got that job that she felt was out of her reach, but, after only nine months, her boss put her name on the list for leadership training.

Patty continues to build more and more positive emotional habits and, like me, enjoys continual expansion of growth in her emotional skills. She is on a correct healing path because she is seeking truths. Every day she practices looking at herself honestly and authentically so she can be the best version of herself.

"I don't care what you think unless it is about me."

— Kurt Cobain

Chapter 4 - Understanding The Narcissist

When I first heard about narcissists and their behaviors, it was more than helpful because I began to see that I was not crazy after all. The strange and baffling things that my ex had done, including how he broke it off with me, made more sense. It was also helpful to know that I was not alone in the experience. It gave me a structure to help me understand what happened and even why I reacted to him in the ways that I did.

It affirmed my observations that the things that he did were not healthy, and I was right to find strange and confusing.

It also helped to learn terms like 'gaslighting', 'word salad', 'supplies' 'flying monkeys', 'discard', 'masks', etc. It helped to put things into clear little boxes so that I could stop my internal confusion.

*

I then joined a few support groups to learn more, get help, and give help in the healing process. It was even fun for a time, laughing, crying, and commiserating with people who had experienced the same thing. It was also sort of a sanity maker to hear about some bizarre things that I noticed in my ex that I thought I must have been imagining because they were so strange. Being a part of a support group for the victims of narcissists was excellent and sorely needed. It was definitely helpful, but only for a time. After a while, it began to change for me.

At some point, I noticed many people in the support groups were stuck in a kind of a loop: a never-ending need to understand their narcissist. They continued to ask one another, "Has your narcissist done such and such to you?" "Did your narcissist used to do such and such?" "Did your narcissist ever say X?" As I said earlier, many of those questions and answers were helpful and comforting at the beginning. But I found the same people repeatedly asking the same questions just in different ways but, in the end, they were never satisfied to move on. They dwelled on it and became stuck deeper and deeper in the pain of their past with the narcissist; it started to be disconcerting.

All the focus and attention on understanding the narcissist appeared to take them no further forward in actually understanding the narcissist. Instead, it seemed to keep them stuck in a loop of frustration and unrelenting pain of not being able to move on. They even displayed great fear about meeting anyone new, suspecting any mistakes of new potential partners to be representing the shadowy behavior of a narcissist.

For some, understandably, having children with a narcissistic abuser makes it a further challenge to move on from past pain. It is definitely genuinely challenging. While that is true, for them to powerfully protect or guide their children, to prevent harm from the narcissistic parent, it is even more imperative that the victim learns how to move on, as it will help both them and their children.

*

No experts seem 100% clear on the causes of narcissistic personality disorders. Most people in the field, at best, guesstimate that it relates to too much attention, too little attention, shaming, abuse, etc.

*

Victims of narcissistic abuse experience a lack of empathy, disregard for their needs, cheating, lying, gaslighting, controlling, excessive criticizing, never being listened to, being ignored, jealousy, distrust, negativity, put-downs, belittling, and constant correction of one's words and actions, just to name a few, from their narcissist.

The narcissist needs to feel in control and think that he or she is on top of everything. The narcissist needs to feel bigger than life, unique, and better than anyone else. He or she is never wrong about anything, and they expect to be treated as a god.

My relationship with my narcissist was complicated for me, to say the least, as it is for anyone else who experiences a narcissistic relationship. It was often confusing and disturbing often. Dealing with the outbursts and anger was painful. I often felt hollow and empty. There was no stability, so I never knew what might happen next.

*

It is easy to want to talk about someone or a group that has hurt you. It can feel good to commiserate with others who have gone through something similar, especially when that something similar was as intense and hurtful as it is being with a narcissist.

It is entirely understandable, but, in the end, continuing to do it does not help anyone. It is like enjoying junk food. It may feel nice for a minute, but then you feel bad afterward.

Belonging to a support group, especially online, can consume your time in profoundly addictive and unhealthy ways. You have 24/7 access to conversations with one another. It can become a complain-fest as well as a see-what-they-said-to-my-post-fest. Before you know it, you realize that you have not tended to the things that are important for your health, growth, and even prosperity, and you haven't invested in the relationships with those who you love right now, maybe even your children.

Your narcissist does not deserve that much space in your heart and soul. Your narcissist does not get hurt by your current pain. You, however, do get hurt by reliving your past pain again and again.

Suffering over your narcissist is a waste of your time, energy, and life. The best choice here is to do the opposite of what your narcissist would want from you: make them become of no importance, make them to mean nothing, forget them if possible. Forgetting them is the very thing that they would fear most in the entire world.

*

Let me ask you a question. What would it do for you if there were perfectly laid out answers that explained clearly all the reasons why your narcissist was the way he or she was. What if there were the perfect answers that we knew were 100% true, and there were no doubts? What would you do if you clearly understood the ins and outs of your narcissist? What would that do for you?

It is always good to understand things that narcissists do. All the details involving whats and whys of narcissistic behaviors do not take away from what happened to you. It does not erase their abuse, and it certainly does not change them. It also does not change your level of healing.

The fact that there is no real certainty about them means that we definitely cannot wait for those answers. We just have to move on and finally have a life of our own without them.

We cannot wait for answers because we will be wasting our lives away if we do. There is no real need to know or have clarity about who and what they were to move forward. The clarity that you need is not about them, but it is about you.

We can move on without answers about them or from them. The real truth is that nothing about the narcissist, or anyone else for that matter, matters to how happy we are, who we are, and what we are doing with our lives, healing included. There is nothing that your narcissist can do to stop you from healing. Your healing, your happiness, and your success in life are all in your control. It is entirely up to you to decide what you want to do. Your focus must be on you, not your narcissist.

*

Put a time limit on your narcissist. Give yourself a deadline by which you will stop trying to understand them and move onto understanding you.

Understanding you is worth everything!

"Codependents are reactionaries. They overreact. They under-react. But rarely do they act. They react to the problems, pains, lives, and behaviors of others. They react to their own problems, pains, and behaviors."

— Melody Beattie

Chapter 5 - How the victims of narcissists are made

I remember a woman asking me, "God, how could you even miss him? How could you feel hurt? How could you feel heartbroken? Me, I would have said, what is wrong with you for mistreating me? Screw you. I don't love you or miss you, and I would never feel heartbroken over someone who has treated me like you."

In response to her words and her disgust at my apparent weakness, I felt a deep shame. After all, unlike her and other healthy people, I was weak and pathetic. That shame that I carried in my heart, the feelings and insecurities that I had gained through my childhood, was nothing new. I had always felt bad when someone or something hurt my feelings, then felt terrible about the fact that I felt the way I did about situations that others — everyday folks, the people who had healthy childhoods — did not appear to feel.

I had to unlearn that very unhealthy shame and learn real facts instead.

Here is the thing, the insecurities and less-than-strong feelings you have, — no matter your background — are not your fault. Don't accept the message behind the fingers being pointed at you because they just don't understand your experience. There is a good and logical reason why victims of abuse feel the way that they do and why they fell in love and felt they needed their abusers.

It is the less-than-loving childhood that has nurtured in you a sense of loneliness and fear of abandonment. You fear being unlovable even more than pain itself.

Most people who fall victim to narcissists or other abuse find it hard to leave the relationship because it is more painful or scary to lose the person than to stay and put up with the abuse.

There is such fear: fear of being alone, fear of not being loved, fear of being abandoned, fear of feeling lonely, fear of not being someone special, fear of not being lovable, fear of not being worthy of love, fear of being meaningless, fear of not being good enough, and fear of being no one.

These fears are powerful and all-consuming. It is terrorizing and petrifying to experience these fears. It can feel like the end of your world. Of course, you would be afraid to leave a person who is treating you terribly when you think that they love you. Choosing to believe they love you is safer than all of those terrible feelings that I mentioned above.

When you feel those terrible feelings, you are not capable of being logical because your mind is filled with anxiety and fear, cutting off your ability to think straight. You can't think. You are flooded with these horrible fears and the way to escape the fear, all those dreadful fears, is to decide to stay. Once you decide to stay, all those fears dissipate, even if you're left without authentic happiness and a healthy adult relationship.

After all, it is still a relationship. And, to make things even harder, your abuser —the narcissist — can be loving even if it's only every so often. Your narcissist's erratic, unpredictable emotional rhythm keeps you holding onto the hope that this could still be a loving relationship. And if your narcissist is the kind that continually apologizes and asks for forgiveness and promises to change, like mine was, then they only help you to further that hope: the hope of a loving relationship.

The abused often blame themselves for the abuse and disrespect. When you were a child and were abused, your caretakers told you that you got what you got because of how you behaved. Once you have grown up and you are with an abusive partner, you believe somehow there must be something that you did or even something about who you are, some weakness that caused them to treat you the way they did.

This means that when your partner abuses you, first, you feel bad about how they treated you. Then you follow that up with feeling bad about yourself for somehow having deserved it or having caused it in some way, just by being you: not being lovable enough, respectable enough, being too loud, being too quiet, being too small, being too big, being too fat, being too skinny, being too smart, being too stupid — any of those reasons would be enough. You fill that senseless void — your partner's unexcusable abusive behavior — with some imaginary fault that you believe is inherently yours.

Your abusive childhood has made you a perfect hotbed for a mean person to be welcomed and even celebrated: a hotbed for feeling bad, then feeling bad for being made to feel bad. Then you feel so worthless and afraid of not being lovable that you think that no one can possibly love you so you must stay. In turn, their mistreatment of you makes you become even more afraid to leave that person.

Whatever insecurities you may have become exaggerated and make you even more addicted to that person. This is why the victims of narcissists often say that they lost themselves and became even more insecure during the relationship.

The truth is that you had a shaky foundation of self-esteem to start with, which was a perfect match for an abusive narcissist to make you feel even more insecure than you were when you started out. If you didn't have those holes for them to grab onto, you would have left them once they showed their true colors.

"Sometimes, you don't realize your own strength until you come face to face with your greatest weakness."

– Susan Gale

Chapter 6 - The myth, know all the red flags so you can avoid them, is flawed

---

When Brittany first came to me, she had been apart from her narcissistic ex for two years. She was over the relationship, for the most part, she thought, but she was frustrated with the fact that she was having a difficult time finding someone new.

She felt she would finally like to have someone to share her life with but felt helpless because she was finding so many men to be no better than her narcissist ex.

Many of the women in her support group seemed to be in the same position. Some even touted that there is no such thing as real love, and that all men are just simply bad. All men act like narcissists.

The truth is that this attitude you hold in your heart makes it difficult to find much good in anyone. Brittany would later remember in one of our sessions that her grandfather and her own son were examples of good men who exist. She had to go back inward, do some more healing and strengthen herself so that she could make it possible for a good man to come into her life.

*

The general advice for those who have been abused by a narcissist or have been in an abusive relationship of any kind is to be very alert and notice red flags so that you can stay away from abusers. Their message seems to be that the reason why you were in a bad relationship is simply that you didn't know how to recognize it. They are partly right but mostly wrong.

*

It is not that you ought not to know the signs of abusive people, but thinking that is the only thing to do misses the mark entirely; unfortunately, that is what most people spend their time doing.

*

In addition, this advice pigeonholes you into the category of weak, fragile, and helpless victim, who has to keep watch at all times in life, looking and ready to find villains. But what keeps you returning to your abusers, at least partly, is your identification that you are a victim. This may sound strange, but most victims do identify themselves as permanent victims with no power, and when you believe you have no power, you then have no power.

In some ways, it is the willingness to take a chance on yourself that actually grows the courage to do something different and succeed at becoming someone different. Moving away from simply being a victim because you were one once, or you have been one in the past, is very important.

There is also something about the act of living in fear. How can you grow when you see yourself as weak and fearful? When you live like a victim, you are one. If that is the best that you can imagine then that is all that you are and can be.

*

It is good to know all the red flags that you should not put up with. But the left brain that knows those things is no match for the emotional reaction that you are likely to have in response to the energy of the charming narcissist, the love-bombing narcissist that will be welcomed into your open and hungry codependent heart. You, with your knowledge of what to avoid, will still be the perfect puzzle piece just waiting to be slotted into the narcissist's puzzle.

*

It's like going into a battle. You need to study, learn, and know the characteristics of your enemy, what they look like, what they do, and possibly why they do what they do, but if you have no weapons, no training to fight, no strength or wisdom, no know-how, and no confidence knowing that you can fight and win, then you will be overcome by the enemy.

No smart general would send in his or her army to battle in such poor physical and psychological condition. A good general would train your body and mind. You would also learn how to fight. You would practice the art of the battle.

Once you have learned how to fight and have been conditioning your body and mind to be ready for the battle, your good general would then build you up to know that you can handle the fight. A good general would not build up the power of the enemy in the soldier's mind so they feel intimidated and doubt their belief in their power to fight and win. A smart general knows that belief in one's self plays a large part in the battle to win. It is the same in any other challenging situation, such as avoiding abusive relationships with a narcissist.

*

It is foolish to spend the majority of our energy and time studying how to avoid relationships: studying, noticing, and fearing. It's like the story of the three little pigs, who sat inside their poorly built house and waited for the wolf just to get tired and go away on its own, but instead they were attacked and eaten.

*

It is a better use of our time to build a strong house of our own, build ourselves into a strong, resilient person, once and for all. Then, with that solid foundation built, you can begin installing all the good things in your life that you can use in the end to beat the bad wolf — the narcissist — easily.

"I used to think the worst thing in life was to end up all alone, it's not. The worst thing in life is to end up with people that make you feel all alone."

– Robin Williams

Chapter 7 - What you really need so you can avoid abusive narcissistic relationships

If you have been a victim of narcissistic abuse, especially if you were abused as a child, you need to emotionally weaponize yourself so that you do not allow a narcissistic abusive person back into your life or fall into another abusive relationship.

The right weapon will keep you safe from the narcissist. It will also train you to improve other parts of your life, which will also empower you to make joyful and correct choices easily when it comes to relationships, intimate and otherwise.

The weapon that I am talking about is healing, discovering, learning, and building life habits.

The emotional weaponizing that I am talking about is doing a complete makeover of your life. You must become a whole new person. You must become a whole new person because you have become a certain kind of person through the victimization in your early life. Living that way as an adult has made you the perfect candidate for being abused and used.

You need an overhaul of that identity that has been yours for far too long. It is time to adopt a self-empowered attitude, be ready to grow, and take on life in a new, grand way. Doing this is a way to receive your birthright.

The most powerful way to emotionally weaponize is to stop being a victim in your identity. You need to move beyond just being a person who is apt to be abused. You need to move beyond feeling powerless by owning that you can have power, and then embodying your power.

You need to move beyond thinking that you are so incapable that you have no power to use because, when you believe you do not have any power, then you do not have any power. You cannot access what you do not see. When you feel so weak, you fall under the spell of villains who appear more convincing. You will be manipulated and controlled yet again.

The proof that only "knowing the red flags" does not work is what manifests in the lives of the chronically stuck members in the unhealthy "support" groups. They educate and reeducate each other on the topics of red flags and the narcissist's evils while they still helplessly return to and have difficulty getting away from them, if not physically, at least, emotionally. All of these stuck people are experts on what the red flags are.

There has to be more. There is more. There is a way for the victims of narcissistic abuse to once and for all learn what they need to learn so that they do not return to the abusers. And, by doing it this way, they will also find the truths of who they are and just what they are capable of.

Let's move forward on a path where you can rebuild your life and heal yourself the right way for all the right reasons.

"Self-love is not selfish; you cannot truly love another until you know how to love yourself."

— Anonymous

Chapter 8 - Radical self-love: How to love yourself

For the longest time, I used to feel ashamed that I often felt less than others. I compared myself to pretty much everyone and always found myself lacking. In my mind, there was always something better about everyone else. Through all of my research, studies, and even training in the self-growth sector, I also knew that I was supposed to love myself. When I would see evidence of my lack of self-esteem, self-loathing, and insecurities, I felt ashamed.I felt like a puddle of disgusting puke.

Whenever I would even think about the idea of loving myself, I was in amazement, complete confusion, and ignorance as to how even to start. I would hear people say, "You need to love yourself," and I would think, "Well, ok, I don't know how and I don't even know what that means."

Once I began to do the real work of healing, I realized that there was nothing wrong with me but that I just had not learned how to love myself. I never really knew what it felt like to be loved or valued. The bad feelings that I had and insecurities that I had were not my fault. They didn't make me weak or unloveable. I was having those feelings because I didn't know better.

The other symptom of not knowing how to love yourself is that you dream of being loved, wait to be loved, long to be loved so that you can feel and understand what that love feels like. You do not feel love or worthy of love unless you believe someone loves you. You only feel like you are someone important if and only if someone is in love with you.

This is why co-dependents become obsessed with relationships. Co-dependents (often victims of narcissistic abuse), THINK and believe that the only way that they could feel love (the good feelings) is when someone outside of them loves them. That is a big lie.

You cannot feel love (good feelings) without knowing how to love yourself. You have to love yourself to feel those good feelings. There is no other way.

Also, you cannot find true love with another until you know that you are worthy of love by loving yourself. If you do not love yourself, you cannot recognize someone genuinely loving you.

Most of us are familiar with the importance of "self-love." We fall into one camp or another when it comes to knowing how to do it. Some effortlessly love themselves while others see that they are supposed to but have little clue as to how. Those who do not know how to love themselves even feel a sense of shame at not knowing how.

The reason why these people feel a sense of shame is because of one critical fault in their thinking. They came to believe they were not worthy of love, and that is why they were not loved as children. And, because they think it was their fault that they were not loved as children and since it was their fault that they were not loved as children, it is their fault that they do not know how to love themselves now.

What they do not realize is that people who know how to do self-love know how to do it because they were loved as children. Loving themselves is second nature for them. They don't know how to not love themselves. Those who do not know how to love themselves, do not know how because they were not loved when they were growing up. They, in truth, like anyone else, were and are worthy of love, always. They just do not know this truth.

If, in addition to not having been loved, which would be considered neglect, they were maltreated (abused or tortured) then they know how to and regularly practice treating themselves with self-hatred in addition to not giving themselves love.

They are highly likely to attract and remain too long in abusive and neglectful intimate relationships. They have been primed and well-prepped by their painful childhood for Stockholm Syndrome and get stuck with equally harsh and abusive treatment from their abuser. These people question their intelligence and decision-making abilities because they are aware that they should not be in these relationships but feel held back by their inability to leave their abusers.

We all have a deep desire for love, so we look for it. When we look for love but we don't have it in ourselves, we almost always attract people who also do not know how to love us, as they do not know how to love themselves. After many experiences with relationships that lack love, that are neglectful and even abusive, we are affirmed in our old beliefs that we are not worthy of love. We see the lack not as what we do not want but as a confirmation that we do not deserve love, making us believe that love is not possible for us.

The answer is for us to know how to and be regular in the practice of loving ourselves.

Let's talk about a few of the main steps to self-love.

Love in action

Love is simple. Loving is simple. Love is action, so to learn that you are worthy of love is to love yourself with actions of love. Begin by doing loving things for yourself — everything from small to large (little pleasures and joys to 'success' in life). Treat yourself like you are important to you.

You were not given love as a child. Your need for emotional and physical comfort were not met. Your wants and desires were ignored. You would have learned early on to agree with your guardians that your needs and wants had no importance.

A childhood lacking loving care can hurt you more than once. It hurt you when you were too little to fend for yourself. It hurts you again as an adult because you learn to treat yourself with that same lack of loving care, thinking you are of little value as you learned from the adults' words and actions toward you.

You learned to go without love as a child. Now, as an adult, you not only know how to go without, you accept that as a part of your life, your destiny, and you do not provide those things for yourself. The way you don't give yourself love shows up in many ways. You might not provide yourself with pleasure, success, financial success and security, good health or a beautiful place to live. You might sacrifice honing your voice and developing who you are to try to please others. You may even sabotage your life or put yourself in harm's way.

To undo what was done to you, to teach yourself how to love you, you simply need to do those loving actions that you went without as a child. You begin listening to and honoring your desire for joy. You take your voice seriously and give importance to it by letting yourself express these feelings. Show your importance by saying no to people and things that you do not want to participate in, something that you do not wish to do. Give yourself love by going after your career aspirations, financial success, good health, and a beautiful place that you can enjoy living in. Keep yourself out of emotional and physical harm's way because you are that important.

Adore your flaws — be your own most adoring parent

When my friend June's third child was born, I remember thinking to myself how far from cute she looked to me. I realize that it wasn't nice. I feel ashamed to have felt those feelings.

The funniest thing was what happened during the following week when I went to June's house to help her with her children so that she could rest.

While I was there, June kept looking over at her newborn and exclaiming, "Look at her, look at how cute she is. Isn't she the cutest thing on Earth?" There was so much love and adoration coming from my friend toward her daughter that by the time I left, I was convinced that the little girl who I thought was definitely not cute before was now the cutest baby that I had ever seen. She looked so adorable to me from that day forward.

You were not loved like June's daughter; in fact, you were taught that you were unlovable. You were taught to withhold love from yourself, neglect yourself, to do unkind things to yourself, and even allow others to do cruel things to you.

Given what you lacked, you likely are your hardest self-critic and the person who loves you the least. That would explain why you remained in a relationship with someone who treated you so poorly. It is time to stop all that NOW!

The next eight weeks are the beginning of your heart healing days, and you will learn how to love yourself by intentionally and mindfully adoring those aspects of you that you would have customarily criticized and found flawed. Not just for the next eight weeks but for life.

I am not talking about stopping your self-growth, self-improving, and growing. I am talking about adoring exactly who you are now, even while you may be in the process of improving certain aspects of yourself.

There is too much to lose by not adoring your flaws. We all have wasted too much of our lives feeling bad about ourselves for no good reason at all. The amazing thing is that when we love those aspects of ourselves, others become convinced that they're great just as I did with June's little girl. Self-love, which leads to self-confidence, is one of the most attractive and lovable qualities of just about anyone that I have ever known.

Be compassionate toward yourself during the tough moments — be your own most compassionate parent.

If you had a childhood that was anything like mine, and the chances are high that you might have, your feelings, especially bad or hurt emotions would not have been validated as if your feelings of hurt were baseless or that you had no right to feel those feelings. Your feelings were either wrong or not necessary. You must unlearn that and learn that you have value and importance. The way to do that is by responding to your emotions with compassion, like a loving parent would respond to your emotions. The fantastic part of it is that your validation of your feelings themselves helps you to heal.

When I was going through heartbreak, I found myself, at first, trying so hard to be strong that when I'd feel hurt, I would be tough on myself about the fact that I was feeling that way. I was hurt over the loss of the relationship. Then I was miserable and ashamed of the fact that I was feeling bad.

I continued to try to be strong and did everything that I could to be strong every time I felt bad or sad feelings.

One morning I woke up feeling depressed because my ex had contacted me the day before, and our conversation was a reminder to me of the loss and the heartbreak. I drove to my gym, barely able to withstand the sadness that was overcoming me. I got on the treadmill with the thought that I may not be able to exercise very long. I just had no energy or inspiration.

When I began walking, I, for some reason, switched from feeling weak to feeling like a loving mother in my own mind. As I saw my footsteps on the treadmill, one after another, I began talking to myself as I would a child that I adored. I said in my mind, "I am so sorry that you are feeling so hurt. I wish I could take it away. I love you. I am so sorry." A few seconds later, all my sadness and the feeling of gloom and depression dissipated, and my heart was light, and I was overcome with a sense of healing. I had never felt that kind of self-healing before or relief from sadness by merely giving myself compassion in the same tone and same loving way that I would a child or anyone that I loved. I was instantly healed because I felt loved by me. My deep parental love for myself instantly healed the feelings of heartbreak, abandonment, and loss.

The way to be strong, truly strong, is to allow love and compassion toward ourselves.

When you give yourself the room, the permission to feel, and be everything that you feel, you provide yourself with validation and the feelings of worth that you may not have known before.

Given your childhood and past, compassion is the complete opposite of what you have had all of your life.

Say "I love you" to yourself constantly — say it like your most loving parent

If you were not loved as a child, it's possible that you were never told "I love you", or if you did then rarely. You must tell yourself that you love yourself from the heart of a loving parent who loves and adores you. Do this as often as possible.

Feel the feeling of love for yourself as you say it as if you were your own loving parent.

At first, when you begin practicing these steps, it may feel awkward and strange. As you continue doing it, you will begin to feel good and begin to KNOW the calm that comes with having YOU as your most trusted ALLY.

If you had less than a loving childhood, as we've already discussed, the level of self-criticism and the readiness to feel unlovable require the complete opposite. You have to reverse what has been done to you and counter the message that has been told to you that you are not lovable. The way to combat it is to tell yourself the opposite: you are lovable.

Be kind to yourself at all times — be kind to yourself like your most loving parent.

In every moment of your day, you have to be in a mode of being the most unconditionally loving person in your life. You have to be there for yourself as the most nurturing adult of your life. You are not allowed to punish yourself in any way, shape, or form, no matter what you deem you did wrong. If you feel that you have made a mistake, forgive yourself, the way the most loving person in your life would forgive you. You are to be loved, forgiven, and adored by yourself during the eight-week heart-healing period and beyond.

You tolerated adverse conditions in your last relationship, which did not give you what you needed and kept you off-balance and unhappy. And that means that you could not have been kind to yourself. It is a Catch-22. If we are not in the habit of being kind to ourselves, we allow ourselves to be treated with less than kindness. By allowing ourselves to be treated unkindly, we grow more rooted in the belief that we are not deserving of kindness and, thus, we are not able to be kind to ourselves. It's a vicious circle. If you had been in a negative relationship for a long time where your partner was often unkind to you, and you allowed it because you didn't know you deserved far better, you need to break that habit now. You cannot heal properly without doing it. To counter how much you have endured, you must now take mindful actions and go out of your way to be extremely kind to yourself.

For every mistake that you see yourself make and for every flaw you see in yourself, you have to be your most loving parent to yourself. You must react to yourself as you would to a child you love and adore.

For example, if you find yourself feeling sad or depressed because of the break-up, you are likely to judge yourself and say something like, "Don't feel bad. You're weak." Instead, you say to yourself, with the deepest kindness and compassion, "I am so sorry that you are feeling hurt. I am so sorry that you are feeling what you are feeling. I love you. You are worthy of love. You are enough."

There are so many ways to be kind to yourself in action, but the most important one is to do what makes you happy and brings you joy. If you love to read, draw, sing, hike, cook, people-watch, do comedy, watch movies, take classes, perform, organize events, go to the beach, whatever it is that truly brings you joy, mindfully give those things to yourself at least once a day.

Sungyun - 8

"Always say "yes" to the present moment. What could be more futile, more insane, than to create inner resistance to what already is? What could be more insane than to oppose life itself, which is now and always now? Surrender to what is. Say "yes" to life — and see how life suddenly starts working for you rather than against you."

— Eckhart Tolle

Chapter 9 - Radical surrender

Radical surrender is not:

To radically surrender is not to allow bad things just to happen, letting them run over your lives and give up any possibility of making things better. It is not about allowing someone to abuse you by staying in their lives and continue taking their punches. It is not about allowing someone to take advantage of you. It is not about staying in a job that makes you unhappy. It is not about letting someone belittle you and control you and not standing up for your rights as a human being. Radical surrender is not about putting up with abuse or poor life conditions. Radical surrender is not about staying unhappy and putting up with far less than you want. Radical surrender is the complete opposite.

Radical Surrender is:

> Radical surrender is about taking control of the ideal outcomes that you want in your life by moving with what you don't want in the most intelligent way so that you waste no unnecessary energy. It's about gaining immensely from those very tough and distasteful situations and conditions of life so that you come out the other end like the most beautiful butterfly that you could possibly become.
>
> It is gaining power and peace by releasing your resistance, being free from it, and giving yourself the freedom to find your own power, like you would with a Chinese Finger Trap.
>
> This is when you completely and totally accept conditions that happen to you and around you that you have no control over. It is about acceptance.
>
> For example, one of the things that will happen to you during this healing period from your heartbreak is pain. When pain comes over you, you will want to try and stop it. You will fight the feelings, and you will feel miserable knowing that you are feeling it. You are in the thick of resisting the pain, hoping desperately for it to go away. Eventually, the pain does go

away, but only after you have paid a heavy price: suffering powerlessly, fighting, and losing.

There is another way to deal with the pain, and it is radically surrendering to the pain. The way to do this is by going in the opposite direction of what you want to do. You will want to move away from it, run from it or fight it. What I want you to do is to move toward it, through it, and let the pain simply wash over you, giving it no resistance. Just be there and observe it:watch and surrender your resistance. Be still and breathe, relax, and watch it dissipate right before your eyes.

The radical surrender method works for just about every negative experience.

Another unpleasant experience that we most often resist is getting rejected. When someone rejects us, our first instinct is to try and stop it because it feels painful to be rejected. We emotionally scramble to find some way out of it or avoid it altogether.

Have you ever tried just moving straight into the rejection itself? I did, and the emotional reaction that I had moving straight into a rejection, that in the past had hurt my heart deeply, was that I ended up cracking up. It was kind of funny, moving toward the rejection, something that in the past would have hurt me. This time, it felt funny, like a silly game. I realized from this particular situation that the heavy and hurtful meaning that I had placed on that particular rejection was partly due to something that was not that meaningful to me. I had thought that I would not want to be rejected by him, but when I moved into it, I realized his rejection really held no meaning, and I didn't care about it like I had long believed I did. I am still not sure why I laughed when I moved into the feeling.

Rejections are amazing just in themselves. We fear being rejected by the very person we may not want in our lives at all That was my case; it turns out. The funny thing or not-so-funny thing is that I suffered the pain of it for almost a year before discovering that I didn't want to be with him in the first place.

What you lose when you don't surrender:

Resistance causes pain and leads to getting stuck. It is like a Chinese Finger Trap game.

When you live your life in resistance mode, unable to surrender, you lose out on your freedom, and become stuck, losing your ability to live your best life.

What you gain when you do surrender:

You gain freedom, growth, learning, success, and the power to affect your life. You gain a lack of resistance to positive movements and an authentic experience with your best potential.

By not fighting and resisting and being afraid of things, for example, pain, you learn a powerful emotional tool as well as answers to something that you may never even have thought to ask. You realize that life does not have to be scary. You understand that life doesn't have to be that hard. You realize that there's more to your life than you knew was possible. You also realize just how NOT weak you are and just how capable you really are to take life on face-to-face.

"Our bodies are our garden to which our wills are gardeners."

— William Shakespeare

Chapter 10 - Radical self-care

Looking back at my healing bootcamp days, which were now about two years ago, the following practices that I implemented have stayed with me. They have become habits that continue to enhance my life. Commit to doing them for the next eight weeks, and the rest will follow. More than anything, doing them will build an emotional foundation for you to heal in the right way and in a powerful way.

Alcohol

Refrain from heavy drinking (during the eight weeks of my bootcamp, I didn't drink at all, and I would highly recommend that you refrain from it during this time and establish a habit).

To heal properly, you have to make sure your mind is clear and you are as emotionally balanced as possible. The problem with alcohol is the day after.

Alcohol zaps away dopamine and serotonin from your brain, so the next day your brain lacks what you need to be as happy as possible. On top of the pain of heartbreak, you will be experiencing an added level of depression. Being free from the depression that alcohol causes in you is your goal.

Drinking alcohol will make you feel worse about the break-up and the loss. You don't need that. You want to know clearly what your real feelings are so that you can effectively deal with them and learn from them.

During my eight-week healing bootcamp, I stayed away from drinking altogether. Even though I often felt sad about my heartbreak and I felt depressed at times, I never felt the anxiety that I regularly experienced with my ex.

With your commitment to truly heal your whole self, you can give yourself a gift of powerful healing by keeping your mind, body, and spirit in their best mode by giving yourself a break from alcohol.

Exercise

The benefit of exercising first thing in the morning is worth everything. Firstly, once it becomes a habit, it takes little to no self-control or discipline to do it. It becomes a mindless act, and, if you are doing something positive mindlessly and effortlessly, you are fortunate.

Next, the benefit of exercising first thing in the morning is that the positive effects of exercise on your brain and your body will last throughout your day. It is like taking a timed release feel-good vitamin that aids you throughout the day.

You will also, contrary to what you might think, feel more energetic throughout your day, having exerted yourself in the morning. I had always wondered why I felt stronger and more energetic when I exercised in the morning compared to when I didn't. I thought it was all in my head. Research now shows that you are able to be more active throughout the day when you've put exercise in the morning.

If you are not exercising regularly or have not been doing it for a while, you can start by doing 5 minutes of something in the morning. Tell yourself your only obligation is to get up and do 5 minutes but do it every day at the same time.

Soon, your body will naturally want to do more. Listen to your desire to do more and add more time to your workout as you go. If what you are doing is aerobics, you can add short intervals of strength training: sit-ups, push-ups, light weights, etc.

You will sweat and feel the benefit of endorphins in your brain. The endorphins will give you a sense of well-being and emotional strength to tackle what you want to address. Because you will start your day by doing it, your whole day will be affected by your morning boost, and you will feel more energized and clearer. You will also walk taller, feeling the strengthening of muscles in your body, which is a reminder of your power and ability to heal. You will feel agile and strong. And, of course, the added and fantastic benefit of this is that your health improves, and a sense of vitality is a tremendous gift to give yourself every day.

I have been exercising in the mornings for many years now because of the benefits that I feel throughout the day. During my eight-week healing bootcamp, I did it every day. I knew that I had a greater emotional load to tackle, and I wanted to give myself an added psychological benefit, like taking Vitamin C to help when healing from a cold. Now that I have added strength training to my cardio regime, I am sold on the benefits of additional strength training. It is remarkable how different I feel just simply walking around during the day. All the muscles that I had ignored are waking up, and I feel a sense of well-being that I had forgotten about.

I know that I could have put myself on a healing path without the exercise, but I would not have felt as fully awake to my whole life if I didn't invest my energy in my body's well-being. The thing about investing your energy into your body's health is that the energy investment comes back to you instantly and daily, giving you back the energy that you need to live the joyful and fulfilling life that you deserve. Exercise is one of your very best friends during this time of healing. And it will remain one of your very best friends long after.

Get quality sleep

During most of my adulthood, I have sacrificed sleep in my life, motivated by my desire to maximize productivity. I kept my body full of caffeine and sugar and dealt with regular experiences of fatigue, sleepiness, erratic moods, low energy, and a less-than-desired level of focus in my work and learning.

Once I began to learn about the importance of sleep in health and even productivity itself, my brain understood it and accepted it, but I still refrained from using my knowledge. Now that I fully practice itt, I cannot talk enough about how it has affected my emotional balance, energy, memory, sense of well-being, happiness, and, in fact, my productivity and mental focus.

Instead of sleeping 4 to 6 hours a day, which is whatI had been giving myself for most of my adult life, I now sleep 7 to 9 hours a night, and I would say my productivity has more than doubled.

The reason for my improved productivity is that I don't feel sleepy during the day. I feel emotionally balanced and even. My memory has greatly improved, and I am able to focus with ease. I don't even need an alarm to wake me up. I now go to sleep early and get up early to get my day started. I am so much happier and at peace, I would not go back to my old ways skimping on my rest.

Eat foods that heal and feed your body and mind.

Mindfully eating foods that elevate your mood instead of detracting from your spirits is a way to nurture your well-being and lovingly and consciously take good care of your body. During the eight-week healing period, you want to give yourself as much mental strength and emotional power to process your pain and allow your natural mind to do its work to find answers and learn things about yourself by eating foods that aid you and give you mental strength.

Food groups I ate and found helpful were fish, chicken, and lots of green vegetables while completely staying away from refined sugar and refined carbs. I wanted to eat foods that kept my moods even and stable as much as possible so that I could think as well as I could under the stressful circumstances. I also took Omega 3,6,9 in flaxseed oil and multivitamins and spent ample time out in my backyard getting a healthy dose of sun (Vitamin D) to help me to keep my mood as elevated as possible.

Focusing on eating good whole foods while staying away from junk was made easy by only keeping healthy foods in the house. After consistently eating those healthy foods for about three days, my taste buds acclimated, and I began craving the healthy foods that were in my house when I was hungry. In fact, now when I find myself getting away from healthy eating and want to get back on clean eating again I simply focus on eating clean for about three days, and after three days I no longer crave the unhealthy foods that I had been craving before.

Keep your body hydrated.

Keeping hydrated is not just good for physical health but also for mental health. I discovered this fact accidentally during my eight-week healing bootcamp.

Since I was going through heartbreak, it was common for me to feel flashes of sad feelings or feelings of depression that would just come on without warning. One afternoon while working, I noticed depression coming on. It just so happens that I also felt thirsty, so I drank some water. A few minutes later, I noticed the depression that I felt had subsided entirely, and I felt a surge of good feelings. I didn't make a note of it then. I just kept on working.

Another afternoon, I experienced depression come on again, and I noticed that I was also thirsty and drank some water. A bit later I felt completely better and felt a sense of well-being and emotional clarity.

After this happened a few more times , I looked over at my water bottle and I wondered if water could have an effect on human emotions. I began researching online, and I immediately found many experts talking about water's impact on human emotions: how being dehydrated can cause feelings of depression. Now, even though I am no longer on my eight-week bootcamp, I always have a large bottle of spring water on my desk when I sit down to work to keep my body hydrated.

"The cave you fear to enter holds the treasure you seek."

— Joseph Campbell

Chapter 11 - Investigate every pain

One of the things that I always feared in my life was the pain. I used to perform the most complicated emotional gymnastics with myself to avoid pain at all costs. When I would fail at preventing it or stopping it, I suffered greatly, all the while still hoping desperately to escape it in some way.

During my eight-week heart-healing bootcamp, I gained skills to help handle my pain. But even more amazing is what I would gain long after the bootcamp about pain and how it would establish a strong emotional skill set and wisdom for difficult moments in my life. It all started with my work to investigate the nature of pain to learn about my wounds.

One of the emotions that you will experience a lot during a heartbreak is pain. You feel a sense of loss, the loss of a loved one. You feel rejected and abandoned. You feel a loss of direction. You feel anxiety if they contact you because you miss them, you feel abandoned if they don't because you miss them. Everywhere you turn, there are reminders of your ex, reminders of what you had, reminders of hurtful feelings, reminders of good memories, reminders of what you've lost. You cannot eat enough food. You cannot think very well. You cannot feel much joy. You are in pain. All you want to do is escape.

What you are going through is no fun at all, but what if you could turn these pesky, painful things to your advantage? What if you could gain priceless things from all the pain that you are experiencing now to make your life better than it has ever been, empowering you so that many of the negative things that exist in your life would now perish for good? What if, in addition to the amazing aspects of life that you will gain, doing this work is essential for mastering emotional skills? What if you cannot become your best without doing this work?

Would you do this work? I hope so because it has been one of the most powerful things that I have done for myself.

In doing this work, you will become the happiest version of yourself possible. And it will equip you with intelligent, emotional tools that you never knew you needed.

This is what you do. You will need a journal to take with you at all times during the eight weeks.

Then the next time you feel pain of any depth, do the following in your journal:

1. Write down the feeling.
2. Next, ask exactly what happened just before you felt the feeling. For example, you thought about a time when your ex said, "You've gained weight."
3. Then ask what that means to you. For example: He thinks I am not worthy of love.
4. Then you ask, what does that mean to you? You might say, "I am not worthy of love."
5. Then you ask, "if he thinks you are not worthy of love, does that actually mean that you are actually not worthy of love?" Really think about your answer. Was he or she always right?
6. Keep asking the questions then, answer the questions until you reach the real facts. The fact is that you and everyone on Earth are worthy of love.

If you have more questions about the above steps, please contact me through my website, and I will go over it with you in more detail so that you understand the depth you need to go into. It is that important!

My website is:

www.healyourheartandfindyourlife.com

The most amazing thing happened when I decided to tackle my pain instead of just running from it or fighting it. Once I decided to tackle my pain, I began to use journaling to explore it.

As I began doing that mindfully, I realized that there was a gift in every pain and every negative emotion that I had. Learning this has been one of the greatest gifts that I continue to give to my life today.

I don't always remember to explore my pain, and sometimes I still get caught up in it. But I quickly remember what it offers, and I stop and explore it, journal about it, or if I can't journal, simply go over it in my mind to learn about myself. It has changed my life and continues to change my life today.

Facing every painful emotion head-on has helped me accept myself completely, become comfortable in my own skin, become one with who I am, and become unconditionally accepting of myself as a human being. I love myself as I have always needed me to love myself.

I want for you to find unconditional self-love, follow unbounded self-growth, and recognize your limitless potential.

"He is a wise man who does not grieve for the things which he has not, but rejoices for those which he has."

- Epictetus

Chapter 12 - Practice doing a gratitude list first thing in the morning

I learned about just how powerful making a gratitude list is quite by accident. I had known about the importance of it from my studies in the self-growth industry and my life coach training. But I didn't completely understand to what extent it was useful until I actually experienced the surprising emotional shift that making a gratitude list can do for you. I will tell you in a bit how I discovered its power.

There is tons of research that points to the benefits of being in a state of gratitude. Regular gratitude practice through journaling or other methods has profound positive benefits for our bodies, minds, and even our relationships with others. Gratitude practice boosts our immune systems, improves general health, and also inspires us to become more proactive in our daily lives. The emotional benefits are that we are more joyful, better able to focus, and have a higher emotional energy level to tackle any difficulties that come our way. We are more likely to grow in our ability for empathy, compassion, and forgiveness. We become more loving people.

I make a gratitude list in the early part of my day before beginning my writing. I find it to be highly helpful in elevating my moods and energy level.

One morning I woke up feeling very depressed. I was having a hard time shaking it off. When I sat down to write, I went through the motions and did my morning ritual of making a written gratitude list. The following list is the one that I did that morning:

- I am grateful for being given a mind that can learn.

- I am grateful for my good health.

- I am grateful for the resources in my life.

- I am grateful for the many great thinkers and doers who actively work, write, research, invent, and create to improve our world.

- I am grateful for getting to write a book that I believe in and am passionate about.

- I am grateful to be on my own hero's journey.

- I am grateful to be getting in good physical shape.

- I am grateful to be strong.

- I am grateful to be born.

- I am grateful for the delicious scrambled eggs that I just ate.

- I am grateful for my best friend, who loves me not in spite of my flaws but because of them.

- I am grateful for the relationship that I get to grow with my son.

- I am grateful for the beautiful music playing right now.

- I am grateful for this wonderful life, for having amazing adventures, and experiencing self-growth.

- I am grateful to be alive.

Right after I wrote out this list, I got up from my seat and walked toward the kitchen to get some more coffee. What was pretty amazing was what I noticed in my steps. I felt like I could take flight. The gloomy feeling that was in me all morning was all gone, my head felt clear, and I felt feelings of joy in my heart.

Since I undertook my eight-week heart-healing boot camp, making a gratitude list at least once a day is a must in my daily routine. Now I do it combined with a seated meditation that I do at least once a day and attempt to do twice a day.

*

I also ask my clients who are getting over some kind of heartbreak, relationship loss, or any other loss, even a job loss, for them to get into a daily routine where the gratitude list is a must.

*

Even while there is no pain to heal from, making a gratitude list is a must if you want to live a life that is filled with your ability to reach for your full potential.

Making a gratitude list puts your mind in a place of limitless possibilities, allowing you to see things that you might have otherwise missed out on.

It also helps you regulate your moods since your outlook in life will be more positive. Making a gratitude list every day will help you attract less negative drama than you may have done before you began this wonderful daily habit.

"A habit cannot be tossed out the window; it must be coaxed down the stairs a step at a time."

- Mark Twain

Chapter 13 - How to lose bad habits

The fantastic thing about positive habits is that they easily induce other positive habits as an effect or result of practicing the initial positive habit. Negative habits work the same way, of course, except for producing a negative effect as a result of the negative habit.

As a child, my life was pretty much about severe punishments, which were the price that I had to pay if I did something wrong. Though I hated my childhood, I learned well how to punish myself for the wrongs that I did in my life like negative habits. Upon doing something wrong or taking part in a bad habit, I would be extremely hard on myself. I would feel like a failure, a weak person, someone with no self-discipline. I felt like that because those were the messages that I was telling myself in response to my failure to refrain from a bad habit. The result was that I never did successfully guide myself out of the bad habits.

I had to learn new techniques if I really wanted different and positive things from myself and for my life. I had to learn about building good habits as a way to lose bad habits.

The benefits of good habits are powerful beyond measure. Habits empower your life or disempower your life, depending on the habit that you have. We all know this, and we all try and try to get rid of bad habits that get in the way of our ability to be our best selves.

Have you ever wondered why it is then that we don't just get rid of bad habits and live a great life? Sounds simple, right? We have bad habits. They get in the way of our lives. They cause us to be unhappy or unhealthy or unsuccessful. We just get rid of them.

The truth is that it's not that simple. Evidence would indicate that many of us do not know how to manage our habits. If it were that simple, we would all live lives full of happiness and success.

We are good at noticing our bad habits. We are good at admitting to them, as well. We are the first to remind ourselves of the terrible habits that we have, and we are the first to let ourselves know what failures we are when we fail to refrain from our bad habits. We can be pretty damn harsh and punishing toward ourselves.

If we take some time out to really think about it, the negative talk that we do likely comes from a place of wanting ourselves to do better, but the result is counterproductive. All the negative self-talk and emotional punishments that we give ourselves neverwork.

It does not actually change what it is that is making you do the "bad things." If anything, the negative self-talk may cause us to take more negative actions due to bad feelings, like feelings of failure.

Think about what we often do when we break our diet and eat something fattening. If we can forgive ourselves and let it go, we may not continue breaking the diet. However, if we persist in our negative thoughts and feel like a failure, we probably will just completely blow it and eat way more than we had planned, so we end up feeling even worse.

And, even if we don't compound on the first harmful act and produce more negatives, years and years of research have proven that humans do not change through punishment. Some mistakenly think the negative approach works because of the times that the negative approach has seemed to alter people's actions. But correlation does not imply causation. The changes in behavior do not indicate a real change but a temporary reaction that will go back in due time because the real learning that is required for permanent change has not taken place.

Decades of research have proven that positive rewards are much more effective in changing human behavior.

So, what does that mean for us, trying to build positive habits to change our lives and live compelling, impactful, and joyful experiences?

We need to use the techniques that actually work to modify behavior. We need to use techniques that work and are a lot more fun, especially as it is healthy and good for our emotional health. Why not use the method that is more fun, lifts our hearts, and has no bad side effects?

Firstly, we need to change our negative, punishing tactics in an attempt to stop negative habits completely. When we screw up, we should acknowledge the mistake, think about how we can do it better next time, then let it go, forgive ourselves, and take actions that will be positive steps toward getting rid of the negative habit.

Once you take decisive action toward getting rid of the bad habit, then give yourself ample positive, loving feelings toward yourself for having taken that positive action. Give yourself a positive, loving emotional reward for taking that action as many times as you can.

For example, if you eat a piece of candy while trying to lose weight, acknowledge that eating candy was not a choice that helps your goal.

Think about why you ate the candy. Perhaps you were starving due to having skipped lunch since there was no access to any other food near you at the time. Decide that from now on, you will prepare healthy, life-enhancing food that you can take with you all the time so that you always have access to it while you are trying to improve your health in the long run. Forgive yourself, give yourself compassion, and know that you are an absolutely beautiful human being.

Then do this. Buy and prepare small bags or containers of various healthy snacks that you can take with you anywhere you go: fruits, veggies, nuts, etc. Once you have bought and prepared plenty of healthy snacks you can take anywhere with you, look at the work you did to take good care of yourself and reach your desired goal and feel proud of yourself. Take it in. You are on your way. Feel good. Then next time you are hungry, you will eat those delicious healthy snacks.

There is another powerful thing that you can do to rid yourself of bad habits. And this next one is really and truly my favorite way to get rid of bad habits.

Take your singular focus and put all of it on adding good positive habits that will take you powerfully toward your goals and keep adding them.

For example, to lose weight for good, instead of focusing on not eating cookies and ice cream — your biggest weakness — begin studying information about excellent health. Add to your endeavor by learning about what extreme healthy eating might be. Study all about the effects of exercising. Research the impact of eating extremely healthy eating and the impact of exercising on the longevity of your life. Learn about how good you can feel and look for a long time. Study how eating well can affect you psychologically, which affects your emotional life and even your energy level for a successful career, sex life, creativity, etc.

Put your focus on making healthy eating plans, make delicious healthy recipes that you absolutely love eating, and do that as much and as often as possible.

Start a support group of people who want to live an extremely healthy, fun, and great life.

Eat dark leafy green foods (preferably raw) at least twice a day. Make sure they are delicious. Eat plenty of clean proteins.

When you eat a lot of those two things, after three days, your taste buds naturally change, and you begin craving those delicious healthy life filled foods. When you predominantly eat those foods, you not only lose the craving for sweets but also have no room in your life for them.

Perhaps you can start an exercise group with other inspired and motivated people so you help them to get in better shape and excellent health. Learn all about the various ways you can exercise and figure out what you enjoy most: running, walking, HIIT, yoga, weights etc.

Begin taking photos of your skin and keep track of how you are improving beyond just losing weight. See how your skin is improving, and, by keeping track, you now have proof of it to inspire you further.

Maybe you can write a healthy life-improving cookbook and, thus, can help many others in similar situations to resolve their problems, struggles, and pain.

By focusing on building positive habits, you gain so much more than just the positive habits. You achieve the results, the side effects of those positive habits, and you can take on positive habits because of the positive habits that you are already building into your life.

"Imagination is more important than knowledge. For while knowledge defines all we currently know and understand, imagination points to all we might yet discover and create."

– Albert Einstein

Chapter 14 - Visualize positive outcomes every morning and every night

When you mindfully and regularly imagine what you want, your heart inspires productivity toward your goal helping you to reach your potential beyond what you knew was possible. When you look at your goal and imagine achieving it and go to the place of feeling it, it causes you to see it as a possibility. This enables you to put the effort needed into that vision without forcing yourself to take action to do it.

Well, beyond the attraction principle, our psychology works that way. We tend to ignore what looks like it will be a waste of our effort, but when we feel its success and can see it happening in our minds, we naturally put effort into things that we had not previously imagined were possible.

Of course, suppose we practice visualizing the outcomes of what we want to manifest in our minds as if they are already happening. In that case, we are more able to continue taking action toward our desired outcome without quitting immediately. When we continue our efforts without quitting, we inevitably manifest what we desire to manifest. That's when we become one of those people who look as if we succeed in anything we decide to do more naturally than other people.

If we visualize our goals twice a day, when we are about to fall asleep and when we first wake up, they are the last thing we think about in our minds and the first thing that we are reminded of in the morning. It makes it pretty challenging to put them aside and refuse to make them a priority. And, if you look at those who succeed in accomplishing what they want to do, it is due to their relentless focus on what they wanted in their lives.

Steven Covey of The *Seven Habits of Highly Effective People* talks about the importance of keeping your focus and attention on your desired life in order to attain it. He tells us that those who do not declare what they want to themselves are less likely to get what they want in their lives.

*

Actively and mindfully do visualization exercises before falling asleep, and when you first wake up.

*

Imagine yourself enjoying something that an extremely healthy and physically strong person would do for fun. Be excited about being in excellent health. Feel the invigorating feeling of being that strong and healthy person.

*

To have an excellent financial situation, imagine yourself doing things that a person with that level of financial security would do. Feel the comforting sense of security and peace as if you already have it.

*

To have a better career or a better job, imagine yourself enjoying and doing well in your outstanding new job. Feel the happiness of having been at that job performing at your best for some time now.

*

To have a great relationship with someone that you care about, imagine yourself spending time with that person having resolved and healed your relationship. Imagined that you are thriving in your closeness because you have healed your relationship. Feel appreciation that you have in your heart because of it.

*

To have a home that you love living in, imagine a home with all its details, walk around, and be in the house that you would love in your mind. Feel the sense of contentment from owning and living in that home.

*

Basically, what I am asking you to do is to visualize what you want in your life that you do not have currently. Imagine it happening right now in its best version, and then feel the feelings you have because it is happening right now. The categories might be:

- Financial well-being
- Emotional well-being
- Relationships
- Self-growth
- Travel
- Health
- Adventure

- Intellectual growth, etc.

Go through each item on your list, visualize what you want as if it is happening right now, and feel the positive feeling you get. Do this every morning and every night.

"It's what you learn after you know it all that counts."

–Harry S Truman

Section 15 - Allow yourself to become a learning addict

Learning is physically addictive. Studies have found that learning releases endorphins, and problem-solving releases dopamine in your brain. It is one of those positive addictions that causes benefits to compound with no end in sight.

During this time of healing from heartbreak, especially from an abusive partner, learning new things has an added benefit. You can fill up your brain with learning instead of attempting to fill the time doing anything else. You are killing two annoying things (heartbreak pain and loneliness) with one stone (gaining knowledge).

My latest favorite learning tool is audiobooks. It is beautiful to be able to be read while you are doing something else. It is incredible to be learning something while doing other things, especially monotonous and boring things like folding laundry, cleaning your house, driving in traffic, waiting for your dentist appointment, or whatever it is that you have to do. You now have a way you can make all that time productive, or at least mindful! You can do those things while learning something new or merely experiencing literature that you had not had time to indulge in before.

By the way, you do learn a great deal from great literature. You learn about history and the human psyche: *A Portrait of the Artist as a Young Man* by James Joyce. Empathy runs throughout *The God of Small Things* by Arundhati Roy. Morality is a clear theme in *The Handmaid's Tale* by Margaret Atwood, and friendship is the subject of *The Adventures of Huckleberry Finn* by Samuel Clemens/Mark Twain. I've just named a few but there are many more fiction and non-fiction audiobooks out there for you to explore.

Another resource for learning addicts is online courses, like Udemy (my favorite), Creative Live, Teachable, Lynda.com, Coursera, edX and countless others. Take classes about Roman mythology or learn how to code… pick up a new language or finally start that novel using the skills you pick up in these courses!

Then there are classes offered by meet-ups and other local get-together groups. We live in an unbelievably rich era of learning, making it easy to become a lifelong learner, to become addicted to learning. There is so much to learn and so much to gain and so much to experience. I definitely feel incredibly lucky. Becoming a learning addict is never a waste of time, but a time-saver in the long run. It helps you gain more wisdom, which is never a bad thing!

"When you wake up in the morning, tell yourself: the people I deal with today will be meddling, ungrateful, arrogant, dishonest, jealous, and surly. They are like this because they can't tell good from evil. But I have seen the beauty of good, and the ugliness of evil, and have recognized that the wrongdoer has a nature related to my own — not of the same blood and birth, but the same mind, and possessing a share of the divine. And so none of them can hurt me. No one can implicate me in ugliness. Nor can I feel angry at my relative, or hate him. We were born to work together like feet, hands, and eyes, like the two rows of teeth, upper and lower. To obstruct each other is unnatural. To feel anger at someone, to turn your back on him: these are unnatural."

— Marcus Aurelius, *Meditations*

Chapter 16 - Hero's mindset

You have all that it takes to be a hero. Heroes have the worst of everything happen to them before they go on their journey to save the world. Joseph Campbell discusses this at length in his book, *Man of a Thousand Faces*.

You are going through something challenging, like the heartbreak caused by your abusive narcissist ex. By solving your problem, you end up learning how to solve a problem that many others have.

You had a terrible and painful past. You just went through a terrible heartbreak. You are in incredible pain right now. The pain that you are going through is your hero's journey.

You are going to figure out what has brought you to this point in your life. You are going to figure all of it out, no matter what it takes. By doing this, you will do far more than just heal your broken heart. You are going to improve your whole life.

As you go on your journey to heal your whole life and find the experience that you always wanted, you will gain the most beautiful gem. It is a gift for the world, just as Joseph Campbell mentioned. And, of course, you will share it with the world to complete your journey.

There is another aspect of being a hero. It is a mindset that you will need to adapt as you move forward. Your journey has been and will always be about real and authentic healing so that who you are changes. To continue to grow in your healing, you can only choose to have one mindset: a hero's mindset. Anything else is a victim mindset. If you do not adopt a hero's mindset, you will continue to have a victim mentality. You can either choose to be a hero or a victim.

You stayed with your abusive ex, who treated you in awful ways, because you had a victim mindset. By going through this healing journey, you have been gaining a hero's mindset.

A victim's mindset means that victims see the bad things happening but do not understand how to use their power to take themselves out of the bad situation. Intellectually, yes, but, deep inside, they don't know, they freeze, and they stay. It's like a deer who is caught in the headlights and can't move out of the way even though they are physically capable. In the abusive relationship, you did not leave because you were like that deer; you could not see that you could leave because your mindset told you that you could not.

The mindset of a victim sees the abuser doing their thing, feels hurt, asks them to stop, watches them not stop, watches the abuser harm them again, and chooses to stay because their mindset blinds them of their power; it makes them believe they are stuck and are not capable of taking charge.

Do you recognize how you used to be in the relationship with your ex?

A hero's mindset is proactive, always looking for a solution without question. Heroes fight no matter what stands in front of them. Heroes face the worst trials and tribulations. When they are done, they do it again.

The truth is that you are a hero, not a victim.

Being committed to your self-healing and self-growth means you have to live up to your hero potential.

"We're not on our journey to save the world but to save ourselves. But in doing that, you save the world. The influence of a vital person vitalizes."

— Joseph Campbell

"The best way to find yourself is to lose yourself in the service of others."

— Mahatma Gandhi

Chapter 17- Move beyond just healing.

Now that you are rooted in a self-healing path, a journey that you have begun to heal yourself in the most powerfully authentic way, you are well on your way to gaining what you need to obtain what you need to learn to equip you to heal your heart for the rest of your life.

To complete your healing and to expand even further into your potential, you must now take steps to share what you have learned with those who are where you once were when you began. By doing that you will be completing your hero's journey.

You can take the helpful new insights that have helped you reach your higher self to help those others who yet cannot see what you see.

Here's the thing…

One of the most powerful, beautiful and magical aspects of true healing is being able to use what you gained from your journey to help others to heal and becoming a part of improving your world. This is your job, a task that you have, and, when you take on this job, you will find true fulfillment in your heart. And, as you find your true fulfillment this way, you will reach potential that you never knew you had. This really is the most amazing part of your healing journey.

*

When we have experienced a significant number of painful experiences, we can feel overwhelmed and helpless. We can feel tempted to fall into a trap of giving up. We might want to take a break from working so hard to get out from under the many things that have gone wrong for us. We could feel like we have the right to give up. It could feel like a well deserved break from useless hard work. This feeling is a huge lie.

The lie is in thinking that it is a break. It is a trap. It is a dangerous trap because, in some ways, our brain is tricked into thinking that it is a positive thing and produces dopamine when we are falling into this trap, but it is not pleasure. It is only a drug that we can get addicted to that gives no pleasure.

*

It does, however, help lose everything important. But, like the frog that starts in a pot of cold water and slowly gets accustomed to the added heat until it gets too hot and dies without ever knowing that it could have gotten out, we must jump out of the trap of helplessness because it leads to death. Perhaps not physical death, but a spiritual one without us ever knowing that we died.

*

I say spiritual death because you may be here physically, but you are not really here and present in your life or are you really able to experience your whole self.

*

Many in our world live in this manner and do not even know that they are doing so. Negative bias is in full swing in our society, and it is just too easy to get trapped. It has become a kind of painful comfort that many live in. But we can't live that way. We can't do it for so many reasons.

We can't since we don't want to miss out on everything that life has to offer. We can't because each one of us living that way further deepens the dysfunction of our world. We want our world to be as healthy as it can be. We can't because it is not our natural state, and we must make things right and live our lives how we were naturally meant to live them.

*

Once you become a person who does not fall into the trap, you become a person who is on the path to master the key emotional skills. And, when you are on that path, there is no way you would want to allow yourself to fall into that trap. First and foremost, you feel so much better outside of it, and you do not want to live in that mode of not being fully alive.

*

By participating in making this world a better place, by sharing what you have learned, and helping to heal others so they can experience a vibrant, full lives, you get to be truly healed in the bestway that you can.

You live the best life that you can, which was, and is, and will always be, rightfully yours to live, by giving back using what you gained to help yourself heal!

I have always thought it the most fascinating deal we have with our universe that the more we participate in the healing and creation of our world, the more fulfilling and meaningful our lives are.

.

About the Author

Nancy Sungyun grew up a California girl. At sixteen, she dove into a life of learning to master her emotional self. Her curiosity about learning theory led her to a master's degree in education at the University of Southern California. Her aspiration to guide others to healing led her to three years of life coach training from CoachU university, founded by Thomas Leanord.

Nancy coaches her clients on their journey to master the key emotional skills, so that they can find their very best lives.

You can find out more about Nancy's work at www.healyourheartandfindyourlife.com.

Made in the USA
Coppell, TX
23 May 2021